Sentence Formation and Exploration

Set III
Book 1

Namrata Dhawle

Made with ♥ on the Notion Press Platform
www.notionpress.com

Preface

Since the early 20th century, phonics has been widely used in primary education to teach literacy across the English-speaking world.

This syllabus is designed according to the Montessori methodology, which emphasizes guiding children through techniques that develop their awareness of sounds. Using phonics, we can effectively teach English reading and writing.

Phonics is a method for teaching reading and writing in English by fostering phonemic awareness—the ability to hear, identify, and manipulate phonemes. It establishes a connection between these sounds and the spelling patterns that represent them.

The primary goal of phonics is to enable beginning readers to decode unfamiliar written words by sounding them out or blending the sounds of spelling patterns. Since phonics focuses on spoken and written units within words, it is considered a sub-lexical approach. It is often contrasted with the whole-language philosophy, which adopts a word-level-up strategy for teaching reading.

In essence, phonics teaches reading and pronunciation through the recognition of letter sounds, letter combinations, and syllables.

To implement this learning method, teachers must begin preparing children in the nursery by raising their awareness of sounds. This involves enriching their vocabulary through exposure to small objects or pictures representing various words.

Most importantly, before starting sound games or phonics activities, it is essential to ensure that children are familiar with the words and objects being introduced.

Sincerely,

Namrata Ninad Dhawle
AMI Certified Montessori Educator
Contact:namrata.montessori@gmail.com

Guidelines for Teachers

Daily Teaching Plan :
Teachers are encouraged to be prepared with the teaching plan for the next day according to the syllabus. This will help maintain a smooth and engaging learning experience.

Workbooks Management :
Please ensure that all workbooks are kept in the classrooms to maintain organization and easy accessibility for effective learning.

Classroom Supplies :
Each classroom should be equipped with a set of **slates and chalk or blank papers and crayons** to foster creativity and interactive learning.

Group Activities :
Group activities should involve a maximum of 4-5 children per group to promote effective participation and collaboration while ensuring individual attention.

Additional Support :
Additional revision sessions should be arranged for students who may benefit from extra practice, helping them strengthen their understanding and build confidence.

Puzzle Words Preparation :
Teachers are requested to laminate and cut the provided **Puzzle Words** separately, ensuring that each classroom has one complete set of **Puzzle Words** (Set II Book 1 - Phonogram) to support literacy development.

Thank you for your dedication and commitment to creating a positive and productive learning environment.

Namrata Dhawle

Singular	Plural

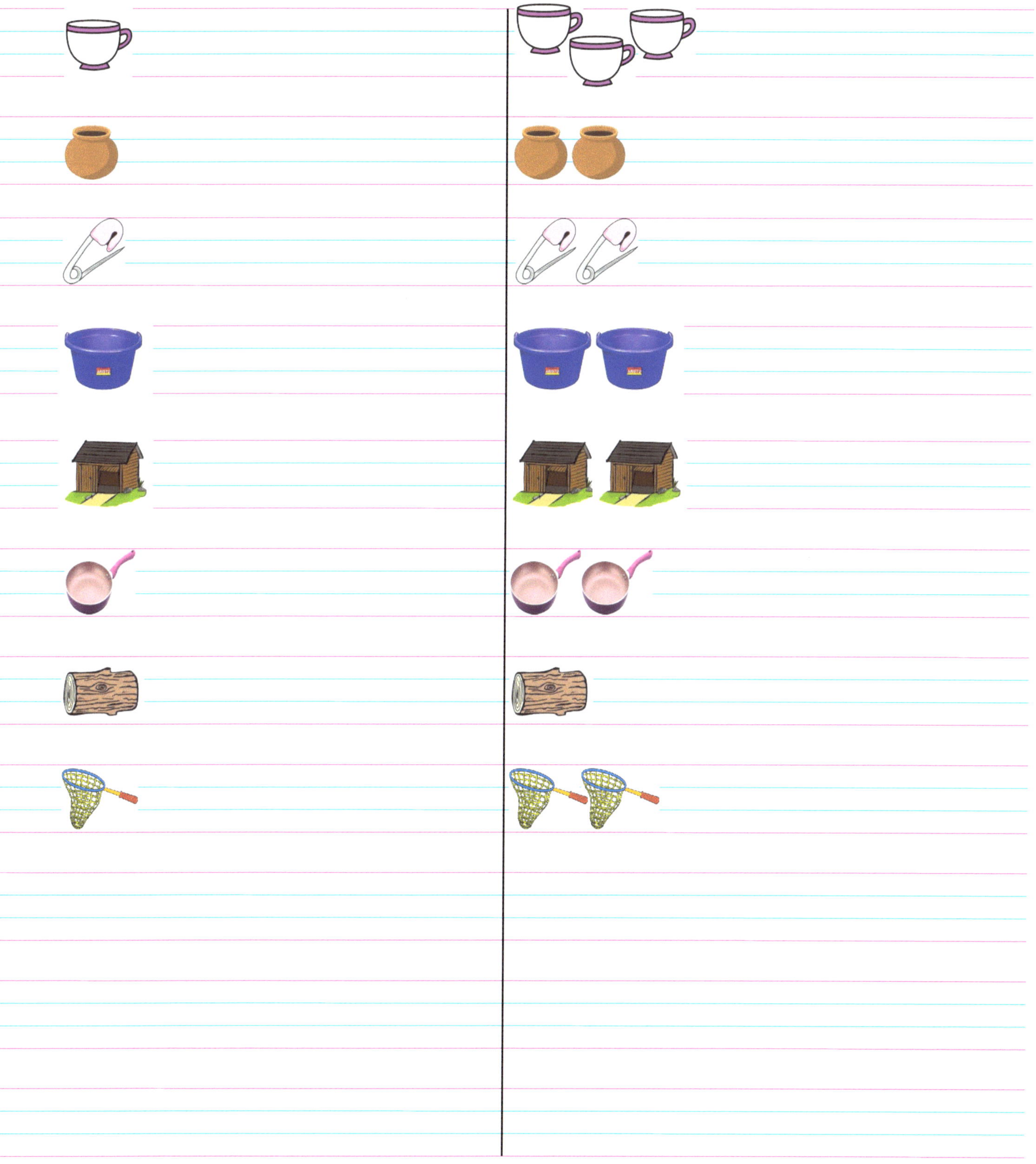

Singular	Plural

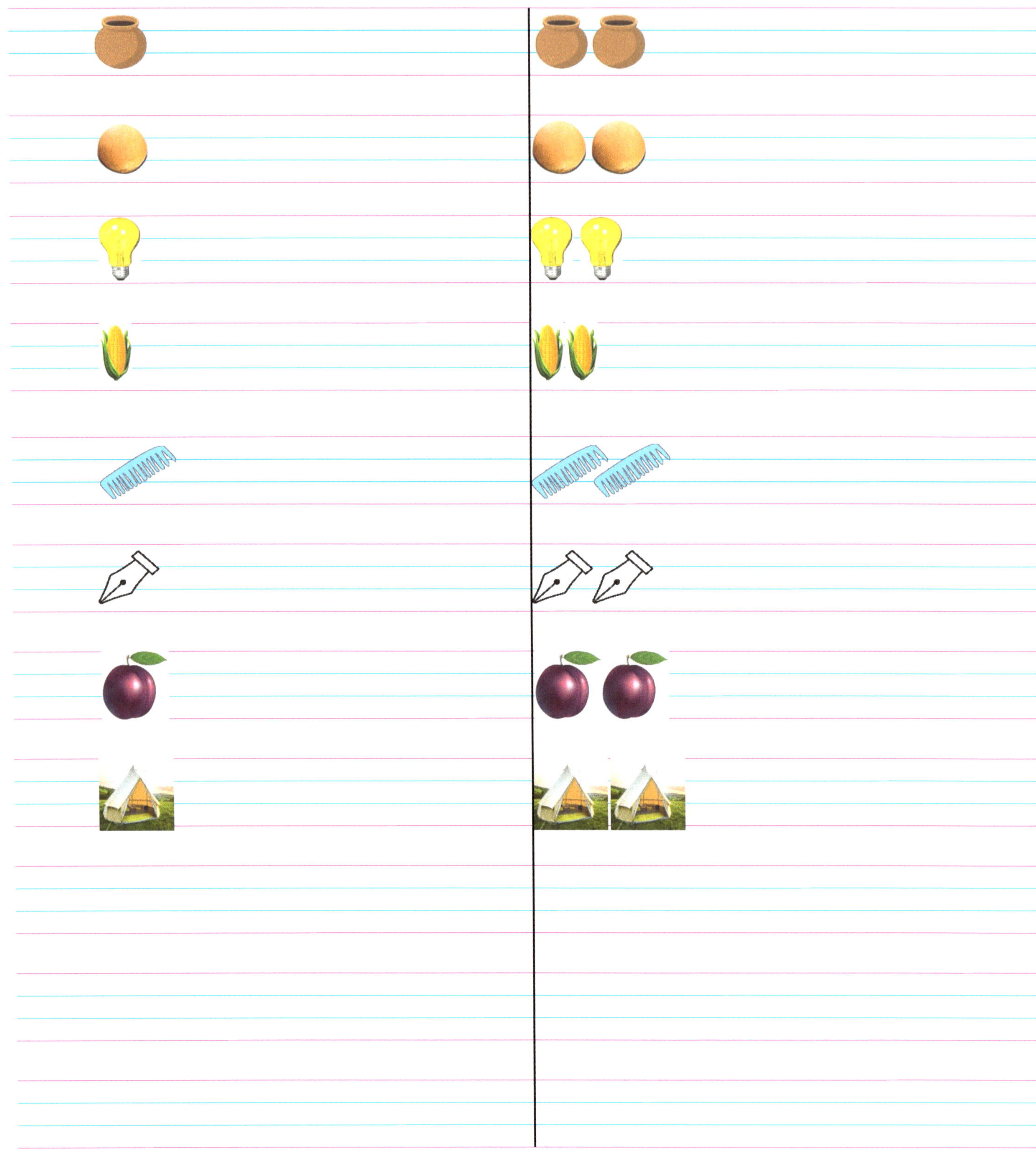

Singular	Plural
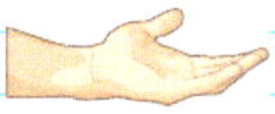	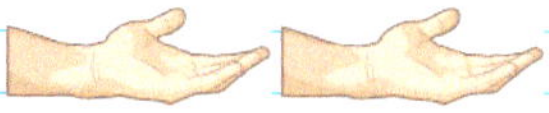
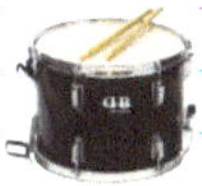	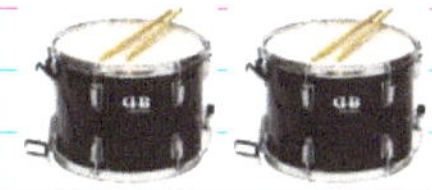
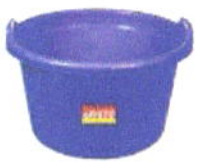	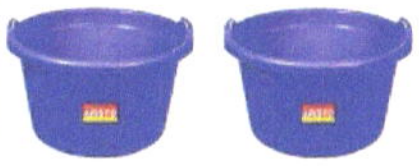
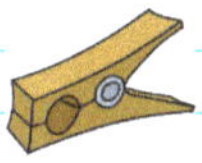	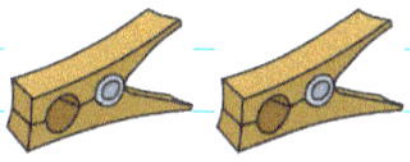

	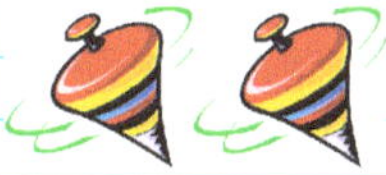
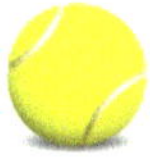	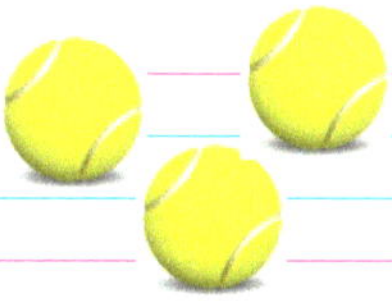
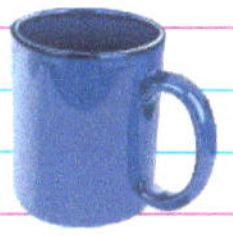	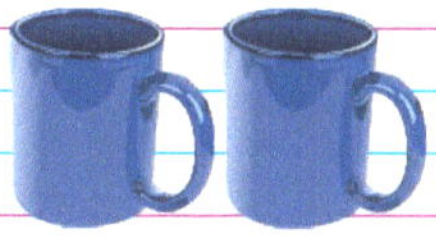

Singular | Plural

Singular
Plural

Singular	Plural

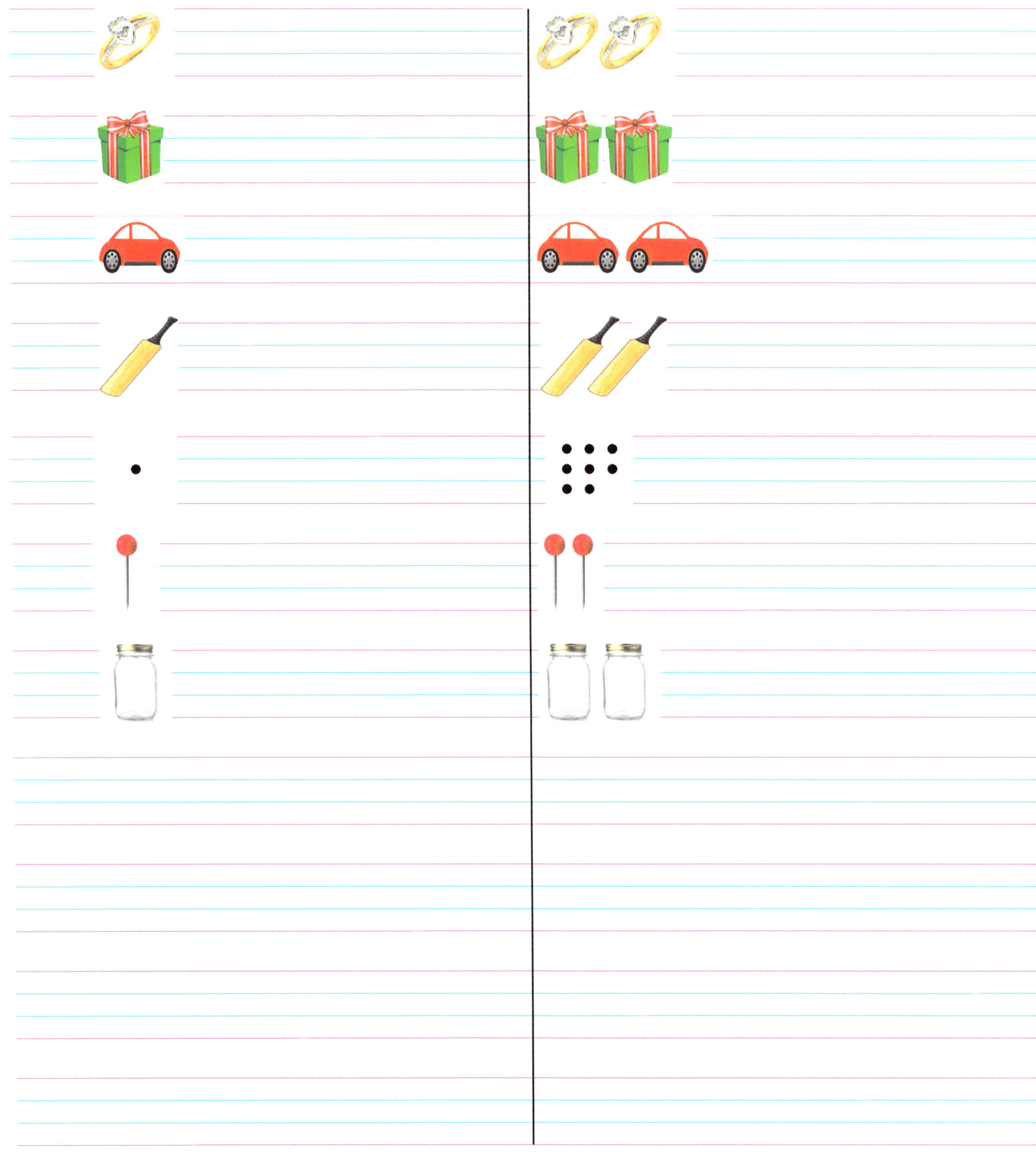

Singular	Plural
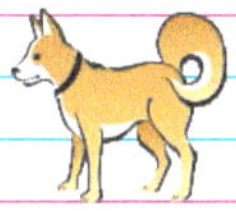	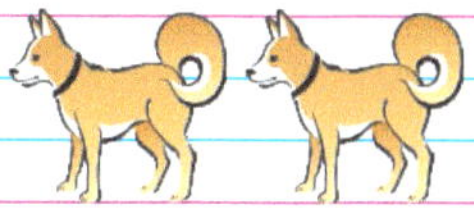
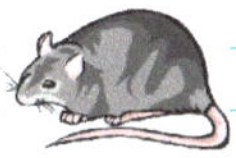	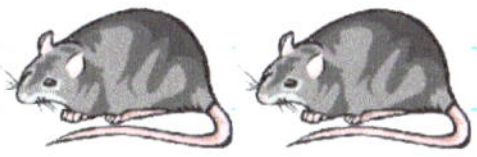
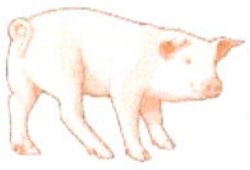	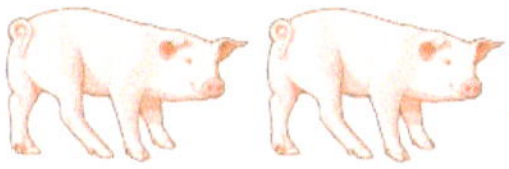
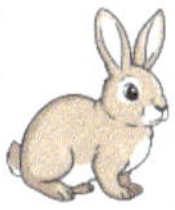	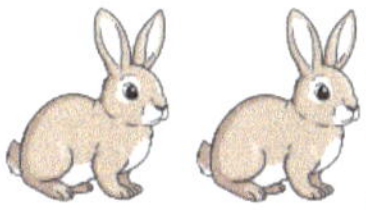
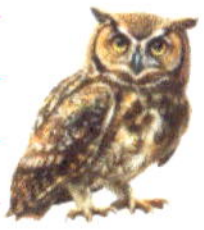	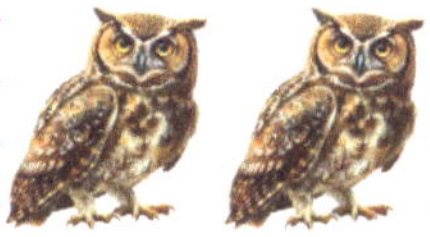
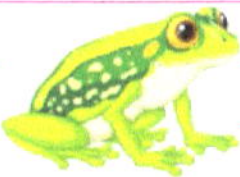	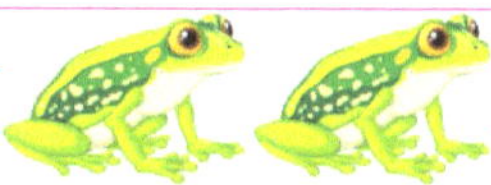
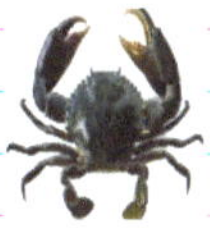	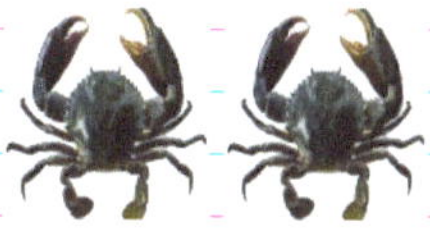

Singular	Plural

Singular	Plural

Opposites

	fast	hot	
	cold	back	
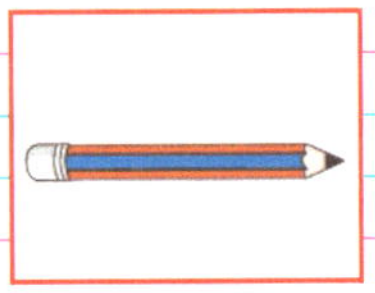	long	sad	
	front	short	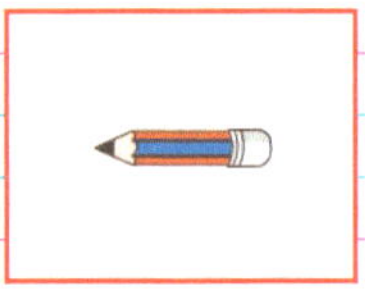
	day	night	
	happy	slow	
	big	small	

Opposites

 tall	short 
 fat	old 
 young	down 
 up	thin 
 inside	outside 
 new	boy 
 girl	old 

Opposites

few	empty
open	many
full	sour
dirty	wet
sweet	clean
dry	close

Opposites

good x

small x

happy x

off x

come x

outside x

stand x

far x

near x

go, sit, inside, near, far, on, sad, bad, big, no

Opposites

come x

out x

hard x

small x

hot x

dry x

good x

long x

big x

on x

go, cold, big, in, soft, off, short, small, bad, wet

Opposites

open x

pull x

come x

stand x

long x

out x

down x

young x

thin x

in, short, go, push, close, sit, thick, up, old

Opposites

under x

stop x

tall x

empty x

weak x

slow x

sink x

throw x

strong, short, go, over, full, float, fast, catch

Opposites

inside x

poor x

right x

heavy x

open x

win x

sunrise x

profit x

close, light, rich, outside, sunset, loss, lose, left

Opposites

new x

dark x

right x

first x

sharp x

rough x

sweet x

fair x

blunt, wrong, last, light, old, smooth, dark, bitter

Distinguish between Bathroom and Bedroom

bathtub, fan, shower, lamp, soap, pillow, bed,

shampoo, faucet, carpet, quilt, towel, crib, sink

Bedroom	Bathroom

Distinguish between Transportation

aeroplane, boat, helicopter, ship, steamer, jet plane, fighter plane, motor boat, rocket, submarine, airship, cargo ship

Air Transport	Water Transport

Distinguish between Kitchen & Living Room

toaster, sofa, gas-stove, curtain, carpet, fork, crockery,

telephone, television, plates, refrigerator, bookshelf

Living Room	Kitchen

Distinguish between Trees & Flowers

hibiscus, neem, rose, mango, mogra, peepal, jasmin, palm, lotus, banyan, cosmos, coconut

Trees	Flowers

Distinguish between Animals (Wild, Domestic, Water)

elephant, dog, shark, zebra, cat, octopus,

lion, goat, dolphin, tiger, cow, tortoise

Wild	Domestic	Water

Distinguish between Fruits & Vegetables

tomato, apple, plum, potato, banana, fig,

carrot, papaya, turnip, radish, spinach,

strawberry,orange, broccoli

Vegetables	Fruits

Distinguish between Day & Months

January, Monday, February, Tuesday, March,

April, Wednesday, May, Thursday, June, Friday,

July, Saturday, Sunday

Days	Months

Distinguish between Day & Months

August, Monday, September, Tuesday, October,

November, Wednesday, December, Thursday, January,

Friday, February, Saturday, Sunday

Days	Months

www.ingramcontent.com/pod-product-compliance
Lightning Source LLC
LaVergne TN
LVHW071230160826
845679LV00003B/948

* 9 7 9 8 8 9 7 2 4 6 5 9 5 *